Cooking with Québec Maple Syrup
Anne Fortin
[Original edition: *Cuisiner avec le sirop d'érable du Québec*]

Project managing editor: Anne Fortin
Librairie Gourmande, Jean-Talon Market, Montréal
www.librairiegourmande.ca
With the participation of *Les Créatifs de l'Érable* - www.laroutedelerable.ca
Food stylist: Céline Comeau
Photography (unless otherwise credited): Dominique Lafond - www.dominiquelafond.com
Photography on pages 36, 37, 50: Albert Elbilia - www.elbilia.com
Photography on page 14: BAnQ - Québec, Omer Beaudoin (1948)
Photography on page 16: BAnQ - Montréal, Joseph Guibord (1958)
Photography on page 17: BAnQ - Montréal, Gilbert Fournier (1954)
Photography on page 124: BAnQ - Québec, J.W. Michaud (1948)
Illustration on page 22: From *L'érable orgueil du Québec* / Citadelle (date unknown)
Graphic design: Groupe Oracio Design - Suzanne Fortin, Gabrielle Lecomte, Claude Pocetti
English translation and proofreading: William Mersereau (Ars Poetica) and Carl Witchel

Editor-in-chief: Antoine Ross Trempe

LIBRAIRIE GOURMANDE
Marché Jean-Talon

Cataloguing in publication data:
1. Maple syrup. 2. Cooking. 3. Culinary tourism. 4. Fortin, Anne.

The publisher acknowledges the financial support of the Government of Canada through the Canada Book Fund (CBF) program, as well as the support of the Government of Québec through the tax credits for book publishing program (SODEC).

ISBN: 978-2-920943-99-5

Legal deposit: 2010
Bibliothèque et Archives Nationales du Québec
Library and Archives Canada

Cardinal / Éditions Cardinal
www.editions-cardinal.ca

All of the food dishes photographed in this book are shown freshly made and were later eaten with much pleasure by the editorial team.

Printed in Canada

COOKING WITH QUÉBEC **MAPLE SYRUP**

PREFACE

Anne Fortin is passionate about everything related to cooking, especially the books on gastronomy that she devours with an insatiable appetite.

Now, fascinated by the sugar maple tree, she shares with us many wonderful secrets in *Cooking with Québec Maple Syrup*. The sugar maple is for Québec what the olive tree is to the Mediterranean basin, Anne Fortin writes, it is "the sacred tree" that is often envied and copied, but never equaled.

From its hard wood, maple warms us, and from its sap comes syrup, sugar, taffy or butter; a savoury sweetness that enables one to discover all the playful culinary pleasures that only Anne Fortin knows how to share and awaken, thanks to her network of friends including chefs whose recipes bring us such mouth-watering delights.

In the way Anne promotes the great world-class food that maple is, advocating its refinement and sophistication in cooking, she pays tribute to all the work done over the years by Québec maple syrup producers and she raises the profile of this honourable, one-of-a-kind product.

This cookbook is a work rich in colours, in flavours, and in tasty discoveries. It's a work that will be in fine company on the shelves at the gourmet bookshop in Jean-Talon Market that is run by our knowledgeable author.

From the tree to the plate, just a few leaves, or drops of syrup, are enough to prepare for us a delicious book about the sweet stuff that we call maple, a pleasure for the senses.

Philippe Mollé, food critic and friend of the maple

INTRODUCTION

Québec is the largest regional producer of maple syrup in the world. Maple syrup is a distinctive part of Québec history, traditions and culture. Here at last it is honoured in a richly illustrated book that includes recipes on the one hand steeped in centuries-old cooking traditions and, on the other, dishes freely interpreted by innovative, world-class Québec chefs.

A cookbook on Québec maple syrup would not be complete without several good old-fashioned recipes from the *cabane à sucre* (sugar shack). The happy springtime ritual of a trip to the *cabane* for the annual feast continues to be a major part of Québec heritage.

As well, in particular I wanted to share a variety of original recipes by leading Québec chefs who are today at the forefront of innovation and who know best how to reveal the potential of our cherished amber liquid with its delicate, unmistakable aroma. I have collected these recipes from my dear friends at Montréal's Jean-Talon Market—cooks and chefs, ice-cream confectioners and chocolate-makers—as well as the distinguished chefs across the province who are members of *Les Créatifs de l'érable*. Of course I must also single out the recipes of my mother who knew best how to bridge tradition and innovation.

Anne Fortin

TABLE OF CONTENTS

FISH

DESSERTS – FOR YOUR SWEETIE PIES

DRINKS

A SACRED RITUAL

THE HISTORY OF MAPLE PRODUCTS reads as a reminiscence of an arduous annual springtime chore. The Amerindians, who did not have the use of metal, knew that when evaporated by the sun or by contact with hot surfaces, the sap of the sugar maple would deliver its sweet bounty. Some tribes would use clay pots to double or even triple boil the sap, and the thickened syrup would also produce a rich taffy-like material.

When the French arrived in the early 17th century, the sap, as a sweet and refreshing water, was the only maple product known to them. Pierre Boucher, who later became Seigneur de Boucherville, was impressed and wrote in 1644 that, once tapped, the maple trees would begin dripping "a quantity of water more delicate than water soaked in sugar, and considerably more pleasant to drink." Forty years later the Baron de la Hontan observed and tasted the sap, asserting "there is no lemonade or cherry water quite so good, nor any beverage in the world so beneficial."

In a later comment on the subject, the baron confirms that the Amerindians were the only ones to make use of the sugar maple tree, from which they obtained both a syrup and sugar already known for their healing properties. Recognizing this, de la Hontan suggests to the early Canadians to seize the opportunity: "As *habitants* of Canada, you could easily fill twenty casks from morning to night if you were to tap the maple trees of your homestead. This little cut does no damage to the tree. One makes with the sap a syrup and sugar so precious that we have yet to find a better, cleaner fortifier of the chest." His words, alas, fell on deaf ears, as he points out "few people seem to have any patience for this task, in much the way many common and ordinary things are improperly valued; there are only little children who take the trouble to tap these trees."

Visiting New France in 1685, the botanist Michel Sarrasin, a member of the *Académie des Sciences*, was the first French person to boil the sap that "runs through the pipes of the maple tree" and to study the amount of sugar that can be obtained from it. It is unclear whether the scholar's work had any influence on the inhabitants, but just fifteen years later maple sugar was being produced in most populated areas of Québec. The *habitants* enjoyed the extra income and, without having planned for it, they caused a reduction in sugar imports from the Antilles.

In Montréal alone, farmers produced for both domestic use and for sale in markets more than 30,000 pounds of maple sugar each spring. In 1712, a visitor noted that the Montréal area was also supplied by the Hurons to the north who were trading in sugar. Baron de la Hontan emphasized that the sap

and sugar could relieve sore throats and most secondary ailments. This power of maple sugar, whether real or imagined, would make him popular in France where, even into the 21st century, many continue to believe in it. A common remedy involves breaking off a small piece of maple sugar and dissolving it in a pint of boiling water—and the healing is sure to follow! Hospital records from the time also show fairly widespread consumption of the sugar, for both dietary and pharmaceutical use.

So which maple products were the most common prior to the 20th century? The sap was not sold, since it was too highly prized and it quickly spoiled. The sugar was sold primarily, since it was so easy to store and transport. Legislation was soon introduced because producers would not hesitate to adulterate the product to increase its weight and volume. Syrup would go sour or crystallize, so it was available only in the springtime, reserved for the sugar producer's family, friends and acquaintances. It was not until the introduction of metal cans, just before 1900, that maple syrup production intensified and achieved wider distribution without fear of spoilage.

The growing popularity of maple syrup was nothing short of a heaven-sent blessing for it allowed farmers a way to increase their annual income during a season when there was not much else to do. The collection and processing of the sap required the seasonal migration of the farmers into his stand of sugar maples where the *cabane* or sugar shack is built. If his sons were too young or if he had none, the farmer camped out alone in the shack through the sugaring season, that is to say, just as long as the sap was running.

In preparation for the sap run, the farmer must bore small holes into each tree and insert a small tube called a spile from which the buckets are hung. During the run, the sap will not wait and for a few weeks there is barely a moment of rest for the maple syrup producer. To collect the sap, he goes from tree to tree. If he is poor, he wears a yoke and two buckets, and beats a path back and forth between the sugar maples and the sugar shack. If he owns a horse and sleigh, the task is considerably easier. The kettle in which the sap is slowly

evaporated knows no rest either. The fire must be constant, the boiling steady and even. The sugar-maker worked very hard. His reward came about mid-Lent when the family joined him in the woods, to give a helping hand. The 'maple harvest' was of such importance in the success of the sugar season that these families were allowed by the Church to break the fast of Lent.

The gathering of the family at the sugar shack required the mother and her daughters to make the best of a short list of "portable" foods: sugar, flour, milk, butter, eggs, potatoes, bacon and salt pork. The primitive kitchen put severe limitations on the cook's imagination. Thus, on the little woodstove, meals could only be cooked on the stovetop: pancakes, omelettes, and preserved meats like ham and bacon. Potatoes are buried in the ashes of the firebox alongside an earthenware pot where pork and beans in sap were simmering.

In the 20th century the sons of farmers who migrated to cities would be drawn back to the father's sugar bush each spring, partly out of nostalgia, partly out of family duty to participate in the labours of sugar-making. On a beautiful Sunday, they would be joined by their children and extended family to take part in the festivities which were crowned by the enjoyment of golden maple taffy on snow.

It was around 1950 that some owners of sugar shacks began a commercial operation of welcoming the public for a set meal as part of their seasonal activities. With paying customers in a restaurant-style business, the maple industry experienced new growth and established the model for the commercial *cabane à sucre*. This has allowed ever-growing numbers to enjoy the annual visit to the sugar shack, ensuring the survival of this most sacred ritual.

Hélène-Andrée Bizier, historian and author

AT THE *CABANE À SUCRE*

TO WELCOME AND CELEBRATE THE ARRIVAL OF SPRING

There are about 7,500 maple syrup producers and 'sugar bushes' scattered in all regions of Québec that are busy at work from mid-March to late April. The temperature needs to drop below freezing at night and rise a few degrees above zero during the day to encourage a heavy flow of sap.

These first few drops of sap into the buckets are the sign that the cold weather has finally given way. In Québec, spring arrives with the traditional, festive trips to go 'sugaring off' and to take in a meal at the *cabane à sucre*, the dining hall next to the sugar shack. There's accordion music, plenty of singing and dancing, and lots and lots of eating...a good old-fashioned feast! On the menu: ham, omelettes in syrup, pork rinds, baked beans, pancakes...

Nowadays maple products are enjoyed all year long thanks to their easy storage and this allows everyone to share in the happiness.

'CHRIST'S EARS' PORK RINDS

Les oreilles de crisse: What a humourous, uniquely *Québécois* name for these salty snacks! There are a few ways to make these pork rinds, but the traditional recipe from the *cabane à sucre* is simplest and best. You'll need 1 lb (500 g) of salted fatback pork (with rind) cut into 1/2-in (1 1/2-cm) slices. Boil slices for 5 minutes to remove excess salt. Drain. Fry in a cast-iron frying pan on medium heat until the 'ears' are very crispy. Dab with paper towel to eliminate excess grease.

MAPLE TAFFY ON SNOW

La tire on snow is true happiness for the *Québécois*.

After the indoor feast, we go outside for that unique delicacy of maple taffy, which, in my view, is the ultimate transformation of maple sap. In long troughs of clean snow, thick boiled syrup is poured out in strips. In contact with the snow, the syrup hardens and becomes a thick rich taffy.

For those who want to try it at home, here is the way to create your own maple taffy on snow.

1 can (540 ml) maple syrup
a large baking tray or bin full of clean snow or crushed ice
wooden stir-sticks

Pour syrup into a thick-bottomed pot or heavy skillet. Bring to a boil and allow to simmer until syrup reaches 234°F (110°-112°C) using a candy thermometer, about 20 minutes. Be careful, since syrup heated to this temperature has a tendency to boil over. Never stir during or after heating since this may cause crystallization. Remove from heat once this temperature has been reached.

Fill a large tray or bin with snow or crushed ice and pour hot syrup in bands across the snow. As soon as it hardens, the taffy is ready and it's time to enjoy: roll up the maple taffy using wooden stir-sticks.

Rustic and delicious, it's a joyous treat from days gone by!

Tire sur neige

TRADITIONAL MAPLE SPREAD

3/4 cup (180 ml) whipping cream (35%)
4 slices of crusty bread
1/4 cup (60 ml) maple syrup
1/4 cup (60 ml) granulated maple sugar

In a large bowl, whip the cream until light and thickened, but still flows well. Pour over slices of bread then glaze with maple syrup and sprinkle with maple sugar. A heavenly treat!

EGGS IN SYRUP

2 cups (500 ml) maple syrup
6 eggs

In a medium saucepan, bring syrup to a boil. Lower the heat and cook until syrup thickens slightly.

POACHED EGGS: In a small bowl, break open an egg and gently slide into the almost-boiling syrup. Repeat with the other eggs. Allow to cook 2 or 3 minutes for soft-boiled eggs. Serve with some of the cooking syrup.

SCRAMBLED EGGS: Beat the eggs together in a bowl with a fork. Pour the eggs into the almost-boiling syrup. As soon as eggs begin to coagulate, stir gently with a fork to ensure even cooking.

Serve hot with crusty bread and slices of ham.

SUGAR SHACK OMELETTE WITH MAPLE SYRUP

6 large eggs
1/4 cup (60 ml) maple syrup
1/2 cup (125 ml) table cream (15%)
2 tbsp butter
maple syrup

In a large bowl, whip the eggs with a fork. Incorporate maple syrup, cream and beat until uniform in consistency. Set aside. In a large non-stick pan, melt butter on medium heat. Pour in the egg mixture, cover and cook omelette for ten minutes. Two minutes before the end of cooking, garnish with a thin stream of maple syrup.

GOLDEN PANCAKES WITH MAPLE SYRUP

Whether thin or thick, cooked as pancakes or as waffles, everyone loves pancakes, especially for breakfast.

2 eggs
1 cup (250 ml) milk
1 cup (250 ml) flour
pinch of salt
2 tbsp melted butter
butter for frying

In a bowl, whip together the eggs and milk. Gradually add the flour, salt and beat until batter is smooth. Add melted butter and allow to rest 30 minutes. Heat cast-iron frying pan on medium. Melt a tablespoon of butter in the pan then add enough batter to cover bottom of pan. Cook 2 or 3 minutes on each side. Add fresh berries or chopped fruit and serve with maple syrup...plenty of maple syrup!

MAPLE SYRUP DUMPLINGS *GRAND-PÈRES*

Despite the name, these 'grandfather' dumplings in maple syrup have deliciously crossed over to all generations. It's a dessert like no other where the maple syrup is enjoyed warm with the softened dough that itself is a bite of maple. The syrup must be boiling at the moment the dumplings are added, so as to begin soaking. Watch out for the hot bubbling syrup that may overflow during cooking–a large cooking pot is a must.

2 cups (500 ml) maple syrup
1 cup (250 ml) water
2 cups (500 ml) flour
4 tsp baking powder
pinch of salt
2 eggs, beaten
1/2 cup (125 ml) milk

In a large, tall pot with a lid, bring maple syrup and water to a boil. In a bowl, mix flour, baking powder and salt. Add eggs and milk. Mix to an even consistency; the batter will be thick. Form into balls about 2 inches (5 cm) in diameter and gently drop into boiling syrup. Cover and allow to simmer on low for 12 to 15 minutes, turning the dumplings over with a spoon halfway through cooking time. Serve drenched in cooking syrup.

COOKED HAM *DE LA CABANE À SUCRE*

This classic, traditional recipe is the way ham is properly served in a Québec sugar shack (*cabane à sucre*) feast. The meat is very tender and the maple flavour is very discrete. At some *cabane à sucre*, the ham is actually cooked in maple sap to impart that delicate flavour.

1 leg of ham (7 lb or 3 1/2 kg), bone in
4 cups (1 litre) cold water
1 onion, quartered
2 carrots, in 1-inch sections
5 whole cloves
1 bay leaf
1/2 cup (125 ml) maple syrup
1 tbsp dried mustard

Put the ham in a large pot, add onion and carrot. Cover with the cold water and bring to a boil. Reduce heat and let simmer 30 minutes. Remove from heat and allow ham to cool in its liquid. Remove ham, poke the whole cloves into top of ham and cover with a mixture of the maple syrup and mustard. Put ham in a roasting pan and cook in oven preheated to 325°F (160°C) for 2 1/2 hours, basting occasionally with juices.

BAKED PORK AND BEANS WITH MAPLE SYRUP

Pork and beans with maple syrup makes us think of the sugaring-off season: the dish is a quintessential part of Québec's rural heritage. Traditionally *les beans* are cooked all night long for the sugaring-off feast the next day.

2 cups (500 ml) white beans
5 cups (1 1/4 litres) cold water
1/2 lb (250 g) salt pork, sliced
2 onions, quartered
1/2 cup (125 ml) granulated maple sugar
1/4 cup (60 ml) molasses
1 tbsp dried mustard
salt and pepper, to taste

Rinse and clean the beans. Cover with the cold water and allow to soak 12 hours or overnight. Bring to a boil and allow to simmer 45 minutes. Pre-heat the oven to 250°F (120°C). Transfer the beans with water to oven-safe crock pot or heavy baking dish. Add remaining ingredients, cover and bake for 7 to 8 hours. Check to ensure liquid covers beans at all times during cooking; add a little water if necessary.

TRADITIONAL BREAD PUDDING

2 eggs
1 1/2 cups (375 ml) milk
1/2 cup (125 ml) maple syrup
3 cups stale bread, cubed
2 tbsp butter

Preheat oven to 350°F (180°C). Beat eggs, add milk and maple syrup. Add bread cubes and allow to soak up egg mixture a few minutes. Pour into a buttered 9-inch (20-cm) square cake pan and dot with small cubes of butter. Bake in the oven 45 minutes or until pudding is nicely golden.

POOR MAN'S PUDDING À *L'ÉRABLE*

The word 'pudding,' which evolved to its current spelling 'pouding' in Québécois French, is associated with 19th century English cuisine. However the original name for this dish, *Pouding chômeur*, or 'unemployed man's pudding,' dates from the Great Depression of the 1930s. With very little fat and plenty of sugar, Poor Man's Pudding was a comforting dessert during those tough times.

Here we offer you two slightly different variations, both equally delicious.

...FOR POOR MEN
1 cup (250 ml) flour
1 tbsp baking powder
pinch of salt
1 tbsp vegetable shortening
1/2 cup (125 ml) sugar
1 egg, beaten
1/2 cup (125 ml) milk

SAUCE
2 cups (500 ml) maple syrup
3/4 cup (180 ml) water

...FOR NOT-SO-POOR MEN
1 1/2 cups (375 ml) flour
1 tbsp de baking powder
pinch of salt
1/3 cup (80 ml) butter, softened
1/3 cup (80 ml) sugar
1 egg
1/3 cup (80 ml) milk

SAUCE
1 1/2 cups (375 ml) maple syrup
1 1/2 cups (375 ml) whipping cream (35%)

Preheat oven to 375°F (190°C).

SAUCE: In a saucepan, mix together maple syrup and cream (or water, depending on your status!) for 3 minutes and set aside, keeping warm.

In a bowl, mix together flour, baking powder and salt. Set aside. In another bowl, beat together butter (or shortening) and sugar to an even, fluffy consistency. Add egg and beat 1 minute more. Stir in dry mixture alternating with milk and mix to an even consistency. The dough will be dense. Spread dough in a buttered 9-inch (20-cm) square cake pan. Gently pour over with the maple syrup sauce. Bake in oven for about 30 minutes. Serve hot.

LEARNING THE SWEET LINGO

If you're planning a trip to a Québec *cabane à sucre*, you'll need to learn some of the maple syrup-maker's lingo, which is quite unique. Rather like the language of wine or fine chocolate in French, it identifies objects and processes related to the sweet pleasures of maple. Here are some terms that, in some regions, might no longer be current.

Aller aux sucres: To go sugaring off, or to visit a *cabane à sucre* during the maple syrup season.

Battée: Syrup or maple sugar that the sugar-maker produces in a single cooking.

Bouillage: The action of boiling the sap to evaporate the water.

Bouilleuse: A primitive type of evaporator, taken as a whole, meaning the boiler pan and the fire box.

Brassin: A granular maple sugar that is stirred so that it will set once it is poured into a mold.

Chaise de lâche: A large chair the seat of which is made with an old burlap bag so that the sugar-maker can stretch out from time to time as he boils the sap all through the night.

Coup d'eau: A sudden, short-lived surge in the flow of sap during the sap run. There are four distinct surges in the run: the surge of the thaw; the river surge; the Holy Week surge (before Easter); and the surge of Saint Mark's Day (April 25). An old Québec saying informs us there are never more than four surges in a given sugaring-off season.

Lichette: A tiny nibble of maple taffy left on the snow. As the expression goes, "Pour on more syrup, because all that's left are the *lichettes*!"

Manquart: A block of maple sugar that has been shaped in a wooden or tin mold. Typically they vary between one to ten pounds and are stacked in wooden boxes before being taken to the sugar-maker's home at the end of the sugar-making season. In the old days they were left at the sugar shack all through the year. Some sugar producers would make 'sugar loaves' of up to 100 lb for delivery to customers within or outside Québec.

Mokuk: The Native American name given to the birch-bark bucket that was traditionally placed at the foot of a sugar maple to collect the sap. Similar containers were also used as molds and for storing maple sugar.

Nombrils: The 'belly buttons,' or large bubbles on the surface of the boiling, thickening sap as it becomes syrup or taffy.

Pignoche: A small cone of maple sugar formed in a mold made with piece of rolled birch bark closed off with a small wooden peg.

Râche: The mineral residues forming a deposit at the bottom of the kettle or evaporator following the boiling of the sap. Also called *sable de sucre*.

Rempli: The volume of sap that is drained into a large container with the same volume as *bouilleuse*, or first boiler. The container itself is also called a *rempli*.

Terminology from the book *Le temps des sucres* by ethnologist Jean-Claude Dupont (Éditions GID, 2004), by permission of the author.

THE TOOLS AND UTENSILS

Andouille: A small wooden plank or tin plate that is pressed into the bark of the maple tree to allow the sap to flow into the container placed below.

Canisse: The large collector barrel or tank into which the syrup flows, coming from the evaporator.

Micouenne: A large wooden spoon used for molding and shaping the maple sugar.

Patte-de-poule: A long, two-'fingered' wooden spatula for stirring the syrup.

Trempeuse: A small, deep-channelled shovel made from birch wood or tin used for filling the sugar molds.

Palette à l'oeil: A palette of hardwood with a hole in the centre used for checking on the cooking of the sugar. The sugar-maker plunges the palette into the liquid and then blows through the hole. As a bubble forms and bursts, if its fragments appear dry as they fall, the sugar is ready to be removed from the fire.

Picot: A sugar mold made of bark.

FRUITS AND VEGETABLES

The strawberry season in Québec marks the beginning of the long summer holidays for school children. What better way to celebrate summer's arrival than to go strawberry picking...and then to enjoy those luscious fresh fruits drenched in cream.

At the end of strawberry season, with fruit aplenty, it's the custom to capture this summer flavour in a harmonious mixture of strawberry with rhubarb and maple syrup.

QUÉBEC-STYLE STRAWBERRIES

1 cup (250 ml) freshly picked strawberries, hulled
3 tbsp maple syrup
3 tbsp whipping cream (35%)
1 tbsp maple sugar

Arrange strawberries in a glass serving cup. Cover with the cream and drizzle with the maple syrup. Dust with maple sugar. Simple yet so delicious!

STRAWBERRY RHUBARB COMPOTE

2 cups (500 ml) hulled strawberries, cut in half
1 cup (250 ml) rhubarb, cut in 1/2-in (1-cm) chunks
1/2 cup (125 ml) maple sugar
1/2 cup (125 ml) sugar

In a saucepan, combine the ingredients and let sit for 30 minutes. Cook on medium for 30 minutes. This compote will easily keep three to four weeks in the refrigerator.

In May, once the maple trees have already given up their last drops of liquid gold, the apple trees are in full bloom, happily presaging a bountiful harvest. Apples are ever-present in all types of Québécois cuisine. The flavours of apple and maple harmonize so marvellously.

APPLE COBBLER À *L'ÉRABLE*

Famous Québec actress **Juliette Huot** was adored during her long career and by the late 1960s she was one of the first TV cooking show hosts and published a few classic cookbooks. Here is her recipe for an apple 'pouding' with maple.

4 or 5 peeled apples, chopped
3/4 cup (180 ml) maple syrup
2 eggs
1/4 cup (60 ml) sugar
2 tbsp melted butter
1 cup (250 ml) flour
1 tsp baking powder
pinch of salt
3 tbsp milk

Preheat oven to 350°F (180°C).

In a frying pan, cook apple and syrup a few minutes, then pour into a 9-inch (23-cm) square baking pan. In a bowl, beat eggs, sugar and butter. In another bowl, mix together flour, baking powder and salt. Incorporate dry mixture into egg mixture alternating with additions of milk. Pour this mixture over the apples and bake for 20 to 25 minutes.

BAKED APPLES WITH MAPLE

A simple, heartwarming dish that can be eaten as much for a snack as for a dessert.

4 large apples
2 tbsp butter
4 tsp maple sugar
2 tbsp raisins
pinch of cinnamon

Preheat oven to 350°F (180°C). In a bowl, mix butter, maple sugar, raisins and cinnamon. Cut apples in half horizontally and core without cutting a hole completely through at the bottom. Arrange apples on baking pan, divide the butter mixture evenly, stuffing the centre of each apple. Bake in the oven for 12 to 15 minutes or just until apples become tender.

UPSIDE-DOWN APPLE PIE WITH MAPLE CARAMEL

In French an upside-down pie is a *tatin*, and this recipe was wonderfully perfected by my friend Ginette. It's an apple *tatin* with all the honest-to-goodness flavours of maple. To save yourself some work, you can use a ready-made pie crust.

2 1/2 lb (1 kg) Cortland apples
1/2 cup (125 ml) butter
1/2 cup (125 ml) maple sugar
1/2 cup (125 ml) maple syrup
pastry shell for 1 pie, or flaky pastry

Preheat oven to 375°F (180°C).

Peel the apples, cut in quarters and remove cores and seeds. In a deep, 9-inch (20-cm) diameter oven-safe skillet, melt the butter, add maple sugar and allow to caramelize on medium heat. Watch carefully so as not to burn the caramel. Add maple syrup and allow to reduce for 2 minutes. Arrange the apples tightly together, face down, on the caramel. Continue cooking on the heat for about 20 minutes until apples are well soaked in caramel. Meanwhile, roll out pie pastry dough. Cover caramelized apples with pastry, making sure to turn into the middle any flaps of pastry. Transfer to oven and cook for 25 minutes or until pie crust is golden. Remove from oven and allow to cool before removing from skillet. To remove, reheat slightly on low to unstick the apples, turn over on a pie dish and serve.

APPLE CRANBERRY CHUTNEY WITH MAPLE

1/2 cup (125 ml) apple cider vinegar
1/2 cup (125 ml) apple juice
1 cup (250 ml) dried cranberries
2 cups (500 ml) fresh or frozen cranberries
2 apples, finely cubed
1/2 cup (125 ml) maple syrup
zest and juice of 1 lemon
1/2 tsp allspice
1 tsp salt

In a saucepan on medium heat, warm the vinegar and juice. Add the dried cranberries and allow to sit for 30 minutes. Add the remaining ingredients, bring to a boil and cook on medium about 45 minutes stirring occasionally. Allow to cool.

This chutney is delicious with poultry, wild game and cheese.

BRAISED ROOT VEGETABLES *À L'ÉRABLE*

Looking for a colourful vegetable side dish to complete your meal? Try these different braised vegetables that can be prepared in no time.

4 carrots
4 parsnips
2 turnips
1 onion, quartered
2 tbsp maple syrup
3 tbsp olive oil
coriander and caraway seeds, crushed in mortar, to taste
2 sprigs of thyme
salt and pepper

Preheat oven to 435°F (220°C).

Peel root vegetables and cut all of them uniformly lengthwise. In a bowl, mix syrup, oil, spices and sprigs of thyme. Adjust seasoning with salt and pepper. Add vegetables and coat well in mixture. Spread out on a baking sheet covered with parchment paper (to avoid the clean-up chore). Bake in oven for about 25 minutes, turning once midway through cooking.

CARAMELIZED ONION WITH PUFF PASTRY

Cooking onions naturally releases a sweet flavour. The maple syrup brings an astonishingly woodsy taste to these carmelized onions.

4 yellow onions, chopped
2 tbsp olive oil
2 tbsp maple syrup
1/4 cup (60 ml) roasted pine nuts
1 tsp caraway seeds, freshly ground
salt and freshly ground pepper
1 sheet of flaky puff pastry

Preheat oven to 375°F (190°C).

In a frying pan, lightly sauté onions in olive oil to release moisture. Add maple syrup and allow to caramelize. Add pine nuts, caraway and adjust seasoning. Spread sheet of puff pastry on a baking sheet covered in parchment paper. Cover with a layer of onion mixture and bake in oven 20 minutes.

QUINOA AND MUSHROOMS *À L'ÉRABLE*

Originally from South America, quinoa is the sacred grain of the Incas and has been cultivated for several millennia. A recent addition to our cuisine, it is especially appreciated by people with gluten intolerance since this grain is gluten-free.

1 cup (250 ml) quinoa, white and/or red
2 cups (500 ml) soup broth
1 1/2 cups (375 ml) fresh mushrooms, quartered
2 tbsp butter
3 tbsp maple syrup
3 tbsp walnut, coarsely chopped
8 green onions, chopped
1 tbsp balsamic vinegar
salt and freshly ground pepper

Wash quinoa well until rinse water runs clear. In a large saucepan, bring quinoa and broth to a boil; allow to simmer 20 minutes or until quinoa has completely absorbed the liquid. Set aside. In a pan, brown the mushrooms in butter, add maple syrup and remaining ingredients. Cook 5 minutes and then mix in the quinoa. Can be served by itself or with white meats or fish.

September colours the maples in the forests of Québec in an extraordinary way, just like the gourds and squash that invade the stalls of farmers markets. Pumpkins, winter squash, ambercup squash, butternut and Hubbard squash are all decorative-what's more, there also delicious when cooked!

PURÉE OF ACORN SQUASH

1 acorn squash
2 tbsp maple syrup
3 tbsp butter
pinch of ground ginger
salt and freshly ground pepper

Preheat oven to 350°F (180°C).

Cut the squash in half and remove seeds. Place squash skin-side down on a baking sheet covered in parchment paper; cook for about 45 minutes. Once cooked, use a spoon to remove the flesh. With a hand-mixer, mix squash and remaining ingredients into a purée. Adjust seasoning. An excellent dish to accompany red meat, like lamb shank (see page 60).

DID YOU KNOW... ?

MAPLE SYRUP CONTAINS ABOUT 62% SUGAR (SUCROSE) AND 35% WATER. ITS FLAVOUR IS DUE, IN PART, TO THE MAILLARD REACTION THAT OCCURS DURING THE BOILING OF THE SAP.

BRAISED SQUASH

1 winter squash or squash of your choice
3 tbsp olive oil
1 tbsp mixed spices of your choice
(cardamom, coriander, cumin)
2 tbsp maple sugar or maple flakes
salt and freshly ground pepper

Preheat oven to 400°F (200°C).

Cut winter squash in two, remove seeds and cut into 8. In a bowl, mix olive oil and spices and drizzle this mixture over the squash sections. Arrange squash on a baking sheet covered in parchment paper, skin-side down. Sprinkle with maple sugar and season with salt and pepper. Cook for about 20 minutes.

MEATS, POULTRY AND FISH

DID YOU KNOW... ?

THE CLASSIFICATION OF MAPLE SYRUP IS BASED IN PART ON COLOUR. COLOUR RANGES FROM CLEAR PALE YELLOW TO DARK BROWN, DEPENDING PRIMARILY UPON THE CHEMICAL CHARACTERISTICS OF THE ORIGINAL SAP. GENERALLY, SYRUPS PRODUCED IN EARLY SPRING AT THE BEGINNING OF THE SAP RUN ARE CLEARER (CLEAR AND EXTRA-CLEAR GRADES) AND HAVE A MORE SUBTLE AND DELICATE FLAVOUR. DEPENDING UPON HOW THE SYRUP SEASON PROGRESSES, THE COMBINED EFFECTS OF TEMPERATURE AND HOW QUICKLY THE MAPLE TREES ARE AWAKENED FROM THEIR WINTER HIBERNATION WILL DETERMINE THE SAP QUALITY LATER IN THE RUN AND THE CHARACTER OF THE DARKER SYRUPS PRODUCED (MEDIUM, AMBER AND DARK GRADES). GENERALLY THESE SYRUPS HAVE A MORE PRONOUNCED, CARAMELIZED FLAVOUR, HOWEVER A DARKER SYRUP BY NO MEANS CAN BE TAKEN TO BE A SYRUP OF LESSER QUALITY.

SOURCE: FEDERATION OF QUÉBEC MAPLE SYRUP PRODUCERS.

SPARE-RIBS À *L'ÉRABLE*

These spare-ribs are a favourite of Rémi and Maude, the children of Céline, our food stylist. They're great as appetizers and can be served as a main course along with some braised vegetables *à l'érable* (see page 44).

3 lbs (1 1/2 kg) back spare-ribs
3/4 cup (180 ml) maple syrup
2 tbsp tomato paste (double concentrated)
2 tbsp rice vinegar
2 tbsp soya sauce
1 tbsp fresh ginger, shredded
1 tbsp dried mustard
1 tsp chili sauce, such as harissa or sambaal olek
2 cloves of garlic, minced

In a large pot, cover spare-ribs in water and bring to a boil. Allow to simmer on low heat for 1 hour. Drain. In a bowl mix the remaining ingredients and paint over the cooled spare-ribs. Refrigerate for 2 to 12 hours. Preheat oven to 350°F (180°C). Arrange the ribs on a baking sheet covered with parchment paper. Sprinkle with salt and cook for 30 minutes, occasionally basting ribs with drippings. For more of a summertime flavour, grill the spare-ribs on the BBQ on low heat.

To make a gravy, pass pan drippings through a sieve and reduce in a small saucepan.

PASTRY-COVERED PORK CASSEROLE WITH MAPLE AND CORIANDER

In 2009, this pastry-covered casserole recipe of chef **Thierry Ferré** from the restaurant **Le Mouton Noir** in Baie-Saint-Paul, Québec, took home the first prize of the annual culinary competition **Les Créatifs de l'érable**. He wowed the jury with his flavours, his originality and his careful, judicious use of maple products.

2 lbs (1 kg) organic pork shoulder roast, cubed
2 tbsp oil
3 1/2 tbsp butter
1/2 cup (125 ml) + 3 tbsp maple syrup
2 tbsp sherry vinegar
4 sprigs fresh coriander (cilantro)
4 cups (1 litre) veal stock
12 French shallots
2 medium carrots
3 large Yukon Gold potatoes
12 radishes
12 white mushrooms
4 sheets of 6-inch flaky pastry
1 egg (for glaze)
salt and pepper

SAVOURY GARNISH
2 garlic cloves, minced
1/2 white onion, chopped
1 celery stick, diced
1/2 carrot, diced

In a pan, sauté the pork with the oil and half the butter. Set meat aside. Transfer pan juices into a small pot, add savoury garnish ingredients and 1/2 cup (125 ml) maple syrup. Bring this mixture to a boil and allow to reduce until it becomes a thick sauce. Deglaze using the sherry vinegar, then add fresh coriander and veal stock and bring to boil again. Boil covered for 1 hour on low heat. Preheat oven to 330°F (160°C).

Place the shallots in aluminum foil, add the remaining butter and 3 tbsp maple syrup. Close up the foil packet and bake in oven 30 minutes. Remove shallots from foil packet and peel. Trim carrots and potatoes into cylinders 1/2 inch (1 cm) thick. Glaze the carrots and radishes (i.e. cook in a saucepan with a little water, 1 tbsp maple syrup and a knob of butter) until they are just slightly crunchy. Trim the mushrooms (use only the caps) and sauté in a pan. Set aside vegetables. In a heavy pan, sauté the potatoes in a little oil and then place in oven preheated to 350°F (180°C) for 7 minutes.

Distribute the pork cubes and vegetables into 4 single-serving 6-inch casserole dishes. Run the pork/veal sauce through a conical sieve and adjust seasoning. Pour sauce over the 4 casserole dishes adding a few leaves of coriander.

Cut out four 6-inch circles of flaky pastry. Place on the casseroles, pressing down any lumps. Beat the egg with a fork and brush the flaky pastry. Place casseroles in preheated oven at 350°F (180°C) for 20 to 25 minutes.

Enjoy with good company!

CRISPY VEAL SWEETBREADS WITH MAPLE-ABSINTHE SWEET-AND-SOUR SAUCE

Ethné and **Philippe de Vienne,** co-owners of the **Olives et Épices** and **La Dépense** boutiques in Montréal's Jean-Talon Market, are great spice explorers who have combed the planet for the past 25 years in search of the world's finest regional spices. In this dish they offer crispy sweetbreads with exotic flavours that make for an exquisite appetizer.

SWEETBREAD PREPARATION
1 lb (500 g) veal sweetbreads
a slice of fresh ginger
1 green onion, sectioned
1 carrot, sectioned
1/2 star anise
10 whole grains of black pepper
zest of 1 orange
1 tbsp salt
1 tbsp lemon juice

DEEP-FRY BATTER
1/2 cup (125 ml) flour
1/2 cup (125 ml) cornstarch
1/2 cup (125 ml) rice vinegar
1 cup (250 ml) white and/or black sesame seeds
peanut oil (for frying)

SWEET AND SOUR SAUCE
2 tbsp olive oil
1 French shallot, finely chopped
1/2 cup (125 ml) maple syrup (amber grade)
1/2 cup (125 ml) veal stock (or chicken stock)
2 tbsp dried absinthe leaf (optional)
1/3 cup (80 ml) dry white wine
2 tbsp dark soya sauce
3 tbsp cornstarch
salt and freshly ground pepper, to taste

After thoroughly washing the sweetbreads, place in a pot with remaining sweetbread preparation ingredients to make a *court bouillon* (vegetable-seasoned stock); by covering with water and simmering on low heat for 30 minutes. Remove from heat and allow to cool for 2 hours. Remove sweetbreads from liquid and pull apart into bite-size portions. Set aside. Sieve and set aside 1/2 cup (125 ml) of the *court bouillon*. (This step can be done the night before.)

SWEET AND SOUR SAUCE: In a small pot, add olive oil, shallot and ground pepper; brown the shallot on medium heat. Add syrup and reduce by one-third. Add remaining sauce ingredients except for the cornstarch. Add the *court bouillon* and cook 10 minutes on medium. Thicken sauce with cornstarch diluted in 1/4 cup (60 ml) of water. Adjust seasoning and reserve, keeping warm.

FRYING: Heat the peanut oil to 375°F (190°C). Mix flour and cornstarch; dip in sweetbreads to coat. Dip the pieces one by one in the vinegar for a second, then roll in sesame seeds. Deep fry 6 to 7 minutes until browned and crispy. Drain on paper towel and then mix with sauce.

CHARLEVOIX LAMB SHANKS *AU PARFUM D'ÉRABLE*

Lamb has sufficient character that it harmonizes well with strong flavours–like that of maple. In the spiced salt mixture, we use Sainte-Béatrix chili peppers whose brightly coloured flakes are matched only by their characteristically piquante flavour.

4 lamb shanks
2 tbsp olive oil
1 tbsp butter
1 small white onion, chopped
1 carrot, diced
1/4 cup (60 ml) of maple syrup
1/4 cup (60 ml) white wine
2 cups (500 ml) lamb or veal stock
8 cloves of garlic, not peeled
2 sprigs of rosemary
4 sprigs of tarragon
salt and freshly ground pepper

SPICED SALT
1 cardamom pod (seeds only)
1 star anise
1 tsp Espelette type chili peppers
2 tbsp fine sea salt

Preheat oven to 325 °F (160 °C).

Grind together the spiced salt mixture. Rub the lamb shanks with spiced salt. In a pan, sear the shanks in butter and oil. Add the onion and carrots and let them brown before adding the maple syrup. Caramelize few minutes and deglaze with white wine. Add remaining ingredients and bring to a boil. Cover and bake in centre of oven for 3 hours. Turn the shanks a few times during cooking.

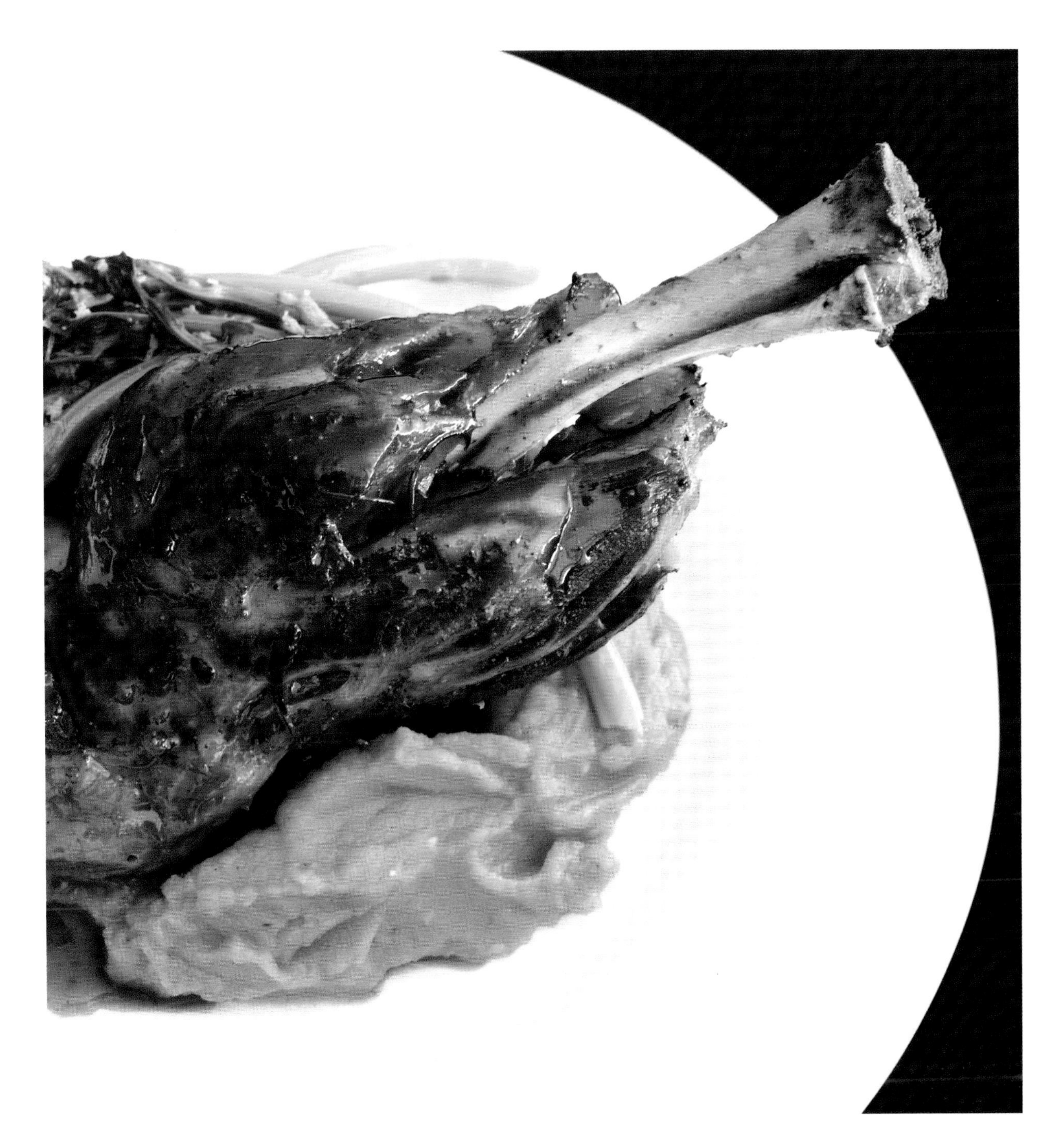

STANSTEAD RABBIT *PASTILLAS À L'ÉRABLE*

To celebrate the ever-growing number of fine maple products that are available for home use, chef **Denise Cornellier** proposes wonderful dishes with these ingredients. The *pastilla* is a fine Moroccan dish that is served during celebrations.

RABBIT
a whole rabbit, about 2 lb (1 kg)
1 onion, finely chopped
1 piece of fresh ginger, crushed
1 bunch coriander, chopped
1 bunch parsley, chopped
1/4 cup (60 ml) maple sugar
4 cinnamon sticks
2 threads of saffron
salt and pepper, to taste

FILLING
1/2 cup (125 ml) dried apricots, coarsely chopped
1/2 cup (125 ml) hot water
2 cinnamon sticks
1/4 cup (60 ml) toasted almonds, coarsely chopped
1/4 cup (60 ml) roasted pistachios, coarsely chopped
1 tbsp maple sugar
1/2 tsp ground cinnamon
1/4 tsp ground ginger
salt and pepper, to taste

PASTILLAS
8 sheets of 'brick' or filo (phyllo) pastry* (2 per pastilla)
1/4 cup (60 ml) butter, melted
1 tbsp maple sugar, finely ground
1/2 tsp ground cinnamon
* These thin sheets of pastry can be found fine food stores or those with Mediterranean and North African foods.

Preheat the oven to 350°F (180°C).

Put all the ingredients for cooking rabbit in a large, oven-proof pot, add about 4 cups (1 L) water or more, if necessary. On stovetop, bring to a boil, cover and transfer to oven for about two hours until rabbit meat easily separates from bone.

Meanwhile, soak the apricots with cinnamon in hot water to rehydrate. Drain the apricots and mix with the remaining filling ingredients. When the rabbit is cooked, remove from pan. Reserve cooking juices. Cool slightly, debone and slice meat thinly. In a large bowl, mix meat and filling. Adjust seasoning. Sieve the cooking juices and, in a small saucepan on medium, reduce by half. Set aside.

Preheat oven to 400°F (200°C). On a clean surface, brush a round sheet of filo pastry with melted butter. Cover with another sheet of pastry and brush with butter again. Repeat three more times to obtain four circles of pastry. At the centre of each circle, place one quarter of the rabbit mixture. Close up the pastillas by folding in any excess pastry. At this stage you can refrigerate any pastillas that you do not plan to bake immediately.

Transfer pastillas to a baking sheet lined with parchment paper, smooth surface facing up. Bake in oven for 15 minutes. Using a sieve, sprinkle pastillas with maple sugar then add crosses of cinnamon. Serve pastillas hot with the reduced broth.

Served with a salad of parsley, tomatoes and mushrooms or a simple green salad.

SPICED-SALT ROAST DUCK

1 duck, about 4 1/2 lbs (2 kg)

STUFFING
2 carrots, finely chopped
5 green onions, chopped
5 stalks of garlic flowers, minced

MARINADE
1/4 cup (50 ml) tamari
1/4 cup (50 ml) maple syrup

SPICED-SALT RUB
2 tbsp maple sugar teaspoon
1 tsp ground coriander
1 sprig of rosemary, leaves removed
1 tbsp sea salt (fleur de sel)
1 tsp crushed Espelette chili peppers

Preheat oven to 425°F (220°C). Wash and dry the duck. Mix stuffing vegetables with two-thirds of marinade. Stuff the mixture into the duck. Brush outside with the remaining marinade.

Mix together spiced salt rub. Rub salt mixture vigorously to coat the skin of the duck. Place in a roasting pan. Bake in centre of oven 15 minutes.

Reduce temperature to 350°F (180°C) and continue baking about 1 1/2 hours, basting occasionally. You can add potatoes and other vegetables around the duck 30 minutes before the end of cooking.

MAGRET OF DUCK WITH CARAMELIZED APPLES AND ICE CIDER

1 magret (breast of fatted duck), about 1 lb (400-500 g)
salt and freshly ground pepper

SAUCE
3 tbsp butter
2 small apples, thinly sliced
1 whole cayenne pepper, minced
2 green onions, sliced
3 tbsp maple syrup
3 tbsp ice cider

Preheat oven to 400°F (200°C).

With a sharp knife, score the fat of duck breast into crosses. Season with salt and pepper. Place the duck, fat side down in a pan. Use the '4 x 5' cooking method: cook over medium heat 5 minutes; turn the duck and continue cooking 5 minutes; place in oven for 5 minutes; then remove from oven and wrap duck breast in foil and let stand 5 minutes.

In a nonstick skillet, heat butter over medium heat, cook the apple and chili a few minutes then add green onion. Pour in maple syrup and cook until reduced by half before adding the ice cider. Continue cooking sauce a few minutes, then serve over the sliced duck breast. 2-3 servings.

PARMENTIER OF DUCK CONFIT WITH TWO TYPES OF SQUASH

"In my kitchen, maple syrup is as indispensable as olive oil, cream and herbs," says chef **Olivier Raffestin** of the **Auberge des Glacis** in Islet, Québec. A member of **Les Créatifs de l'érable** culinary group, he created this parmentier (a dish akin to shepherd's pie) that is as pleasing to the eye as it is delicious to eat.

1 small butternut squash
1 small spaghetti squash
1/4 cup + 3 tbsp (100 ml) olive oil
1 sprig of thyme
1 branch of fresh rosemary
2 French shallots, minced
1/2 cup (150 ml) maple porto (either *Charles-Aimé Robert du Domaine Acer* or *Sortilège* brands)
1 1/4 cups (300 ml) veal or duck broth
salt and pepper to taste
duck leg confit (2 legs, deboned)

Preheat oven to 300°F (150°C).

Cut both squashes in two, from top to bottom. Remove seeds. Drizzle with olive oil. Season with salt and pepper; add a sprig of fresh thyme. Bake in oven, covered, about 1 hour. Remove flesh from squash skins, keeping separate. Purée the butternut squash in a food processor or with a fork. Set aside.

In a saucepan, place the shallots with the maple porto and rosemary. Bring to a boil and reduce by two thirds. Add veal broth and bring to a boil again. Adjust seasoning. Put everything through a sieve.

Preheat oven to 400°F (200°C). Use a cylinder 3 inches (8 cm) in diameter as a mold (i.e. you can use a metal can with the lids removed). First place shredded spaghetti squash (the lightest colour). Add a layer of duck confit. Cover with butternut squash. Remove the cylinder. Bake 5 minutes. Serve with vegetables, cipollini onions and pieces of bacon. Spoon with warm sauce. 2-3 servings.

SPICY CHICKEN WITH MAPLE

Marie-Fleur St-Pierre, the young chef of **Tapeo**, a restaurant that everyone must try in the Villeray district of Montréal, offers tapas of all kinds: some highly authentic, inspired by the hot Mediterranean sun, as well as others that feature the bold, rustic flavours of a springtime in Québec.

6 chicken wings, halved
6 tbsp chicken drumsticks
3 tbsp spice mixture: smoked paprika, cumin, coriander
a dash of olive oil
2 tbsp brandy or sherry (optional)
1/4 cup (60 ml) maple syrup
pinch of salt

Grind the spices together. Using a sharp knife, make cuts to the chicken pieces and place them in a bowl. Drizzle with olive oil and a pinch of salt. Add the brandy, spices and maple syrup. Stir to coat chicken pieces. Cover and refrigerate for 2 to 12 hours.

Preheat oven to 375°F (190°C). Place chicken pieces on a baking sheet lined with parchment paper. Bake 30 minutes or more, depending on size of pieces, turning halfway through cooking.

CHICKEN WITH CRANBERRY, THYME AND MAPLE

Louise Gagnon, a contributor to *Châtelaine* magazine, a popular monthly in Québec, cooks this chicken dish which harmonizes the sweetness of maple and the sourness of cranberry. Quick to prepare, it will please the whole family.

4 skinless chicken thighs
4 tbsp of all-purpose flour
2 tbsp olive oil
2 sprigs fresh thyme
2 onions, chopped
2 cups (500 ml) fresh or frozen cranberries
1 cup (250 ml) apple juice
2/3 cup (150 ml) maple syrup
salt and pepper

Preheat oven to 375°F (190°C).

Flour the chicken legs and shake well to remove the excess. In a nonstick skillet, brown the legs in oil, then place in a Pyrex dish or roasting pan. Add the thyme, onions, cranberries, apple juice and the maple syrup; season with salt and pepper. Bake in oven, uncovered, about 75 minutes, turning halfway through cooking.

QUAIL WITH MAPLE SYRUP AND BALSAMIC VINEGAR

Quail is much smaller and less fatty than chicken. Depending on its size, calculate about one and a half quail per person. To ensure that this simple recipe is a gourmet success, **Michel Boulais** of the butcher shop **Prince Noir** at Montréal's Jean-Talon Market recommends using a very high quality balsamic vinegar.

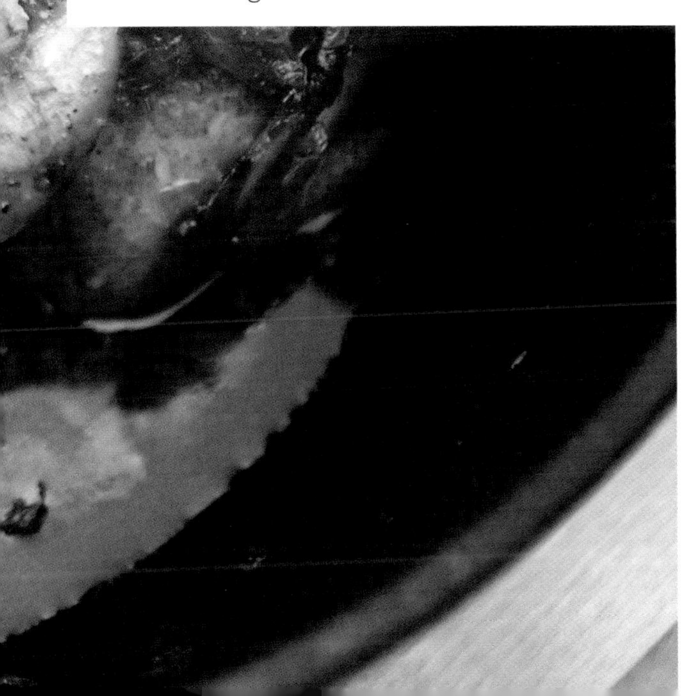

6 quail
1 large onion, chopped

MARINADE
1/2 cup (125 ml) olive oil
4 tbsp maple syrup
1 tbsp Dijon mustard
1 tbsp fine balsamic vinegar
1 tsp ground ginger

Mix marinade ingredients together in a bowl and marinate the quail for 40 minutes, turning every 10 minutes. Preheat oven to 350°F (180°C). In a large oven-safe skillet, sauté onion in 4 tbsp oil on stovetop. Add the quail and brown on all sides. Pour over the marinade and bake quail uncovered in oven for 45 minutes.

WARM SMOKE-HOUSE COD

The art of smoking fish means harmonizing the maple sugar, the salt and the exquisite flavours of cod. The fish should be as fresh as possible in order to retain its flavours.

4 cod fillets of 1/3 lb (150g) each
2 tbsp maple sugar
1 tbsp sea salt
1 tsp freshly ground black pepper
1/2 cup (125 ml) sugar maple wood chips
(or other aromatic woods)
1 tbsp olive oil
1 tbsp of maple sugar (optional)

Season the cod fillets with maple sugar, salt, pepper and refrigerate 2 hours. Soak wood chips in a bowl of fresh water for 2 hours. Drain chips and place them in a pot the bottom of which has been lined with foil. Install a small grill raised over the wood chips. Put lid on, turn oven hood fan on maximum, then heat on medium for 5 minutes.

Meanwhile, rinse the fillets briefly under cold running water and pat dry. Coat the fillets with olive oil and sprinkle, if desired, with maple sugar. When there is enough smoke in the pot, place fillets on grill and reduce heat. Cook for 5 minutes, then extinguish the fire. Allow to stand in closed pot for another 5 to 10 minutes.

Serve with a green salad and Maple Vinaigrette, a creation of Jérôme Ferrer that goes excellently with the flavours of smoked cod.

MAPLE VINAIGRETTE

1 apple (McIntosh or Cortland)
1/3 cup (80 ml) maple syrup
1/3 cup (80 ml) apple cider vinegar
1 cup olive oil
1/4 cup (60 ml) apple cider
salt and pepper

Peel and core the apple. Mix the apple, maple syrup and cider vinegar in a blender. Make an emulsion by adding the oil and apple cider. Season with salt and pepper.

SALMON WITH SPICE CRUST

This salmon takes on the gold colour of maple. What a winning flavour combination!

4 salmon fillets, 6 oz (150 g) each
1/4 cup (60 ml) maple syrup
zest of a lemon or orange
2 tbsp mustard seeds
1 tbsp coriander seeds
1 tbsp fennel seeds
2 tsp sea salt
a long pepper or 1 tsp ground black pepper
2 tbsp olive oil

Preheat oven to 400°F (200°C).

In a small saucepan, reduce the maple syrup mixed with lemon zest by a third, let cool and strain. In a mortar, coarsely grind the spices and empty onto a plate. Brush the flesh of the salmon fillets with reduced maple syrup and coat with spice mixture. In an oven-safe skillet, heat oil and sear salmon fillets 2 minutes per side. Bake in oven about 8 minutes or less, according to taste.

GRAVLAX *À L'ÉRABLE*

With the sophistication of sushi, this raw salmon specialty of Scandinavian origin has lively herb flavours combined with a woody sugar-maple marinade.

a salmon fillet of 1 kg (2.2 lb), with skin, cut in 2 lengthwise
4 tbsp maple sugar
4 tbsp coarse sea salt
2 tbsp white pepper
1 bunch fresh dill, chopped
2 tbsp maple liqueur Val Robert (optional)

In a bowl, combine the maple sugar, salt, pepper, dill and maple liqueur. Place first half of salmon fillet in a dish, skin-side down. Spread salt-dill mixture evenly over fillet and then cover with the second fillet, skin-side up. Cover with plastic wrap and put a weight on the fillets (e.g. a brick, heavy box, etc.). Refrigerate 2 days, taking care to turn the fish a few times to ensure that it is well marinated. After 2 days rinse thoroughly under running water to remove the marinade. Blot thoroughly. Slice thinly and serve.

FOR YOUR SWEETIE PIES

Fait
à la main
Fait
à la main

OLD-FASHIONED MAPLE SYRUP PIE

For those interested in French Canadian cooking, look no further than **Lorraine Boisvenue**'s *Le Guide de la cuisine traditionnelle québécoise*, originally published in 1979. It documents centuries of Québec's rich culinary history.

The choice of this maple syrup pie recipe is not random; it is the one for which Madame Boisvenue has received the most comments over the years. Countless readers have remarked, "So this is my grandmother's long-lost recipe!"

2 tbsp butter
4 tbsp flour
1 cup (250 ml) maple syrup
1/2 cup (125 ml) water
1/2 cup (125 ml) chopped walnuts
1 unbaked pie crust

Preheat oven to 350°F (175°C).

Melt butter, add flour and cook, stirring until the mixture is a beautiful brown. Add maple syrup and water and cook, stirring until thickened. Let cool and stir in nuts. Pour into unbaked pie crust. Bake for about 30 minutes.

DID YOU KNOW... ?

PRODUCTS SUCH AS MAPLE TAFFY, MAPLE SUGAR AND MAPLE BUTTER ARE THE SIMPLE RESULTS OF LONG COOKING. NO ADDITIVES ARE ADDED.

MAPLE SQUARES

Just a small piece of one of these squares will satisfy your sweet tooth for a good long time!

SYRUP
1/2 cup (125 ml) maple sugar or brown sugar
1 1/2 cups (375 ml) maple syrup

CRUST
1 1/2 cups (375 ml) all-purpose flour
1/4 cup (60 ml) brown sugar
1/2 cup (125 ml) butter

BATTER
3 eggs, beaten
3 tbsp all-purpose flour
pinch of salt
1/2 tsp vanilla

Preheat oven to 400°F (200°C).

In a saucepan, prepare the syrup by simmering the maple or brown sugar with maple syrup for 5 minutes; cool. In a bowl, combine the crust ingredients until just mixed. Press lightly into a greased 9 inch (23-cm) square pan. Bake 10 minutes. Remove from oven and reduce temperature to 350°F (180°C). In a bowl, whisk eggs and add the warm syrup, whisking vigorously. Add remaining ingredients. Pour over baked crust.
Bake for about 25 minutes.

MAPLE COOKIES

Traditionally, vegetable shortening was the fat used by Québec cooks for baking cakes, pies and cookies.

Here is an old farm recipe for maple cookies that has brought happiness to thousands of children as an after-school snack.

1/2 cup (125 ml) vegetable shortening or butter, softened
1 egg
1 cup (250 ml) maple syrup
1/2 cup (125 ml) milk
1 1/2 cups (375 ml) flour
1 1/2 cups (375 ml) oat flour
2 tsp baking powder
1 tsp salt
1 tsp nutmeg
1 cup chopped walnuts

Preheat oven to 375°F (190°C).

Whip shortening or butter until creamy. Gradually add egg, maple syrup and milk. In a bowl, combine flours, baking powder, salt and nutmeg. Stir the liquid ingredients into dry ingredients and add nuts. Drop by spoonfuls onto a well-buttered baking sheet. Bake about 15 minutes.

MAPLE LAYER CAKE

Germaine Gloutnez was director of a school of 'home economics' in the 1950s and trained several generations of Québec cooks. In 1979 she published *La Cuisine québécoise* that quickly became a bestseller. From the book, here is her maple cake that has inspired homemakers for decades.

1/2 cup (100 g) butter
1/2 cup (110 g) sugar
2 eggs
3 cups (750 ml) pastry flour
3 tsp baking powder
1 tsp salt
1 cup (250 ml) maple syrup
1/2 cup (125 ml) milk

Preheat oven to 350°F (180°C).

Grease two round 9-inch (23 cm) cake pans and line with brown paper; grease the paper. Cream the butter; add sugar then eggs one at a time, beating to keep a light mixture. Sift together dry ingredients. Mix together milk and maple syrup. Begin adding dry and wet ingredients to butter mixture in alternating fashion, beginning and ending with dry ingredients. Pour batter into prepared pans. Bake 30-35 minutes. Cool and top with maple icing (see below).

MAPLE ICING

6 tbsp (90 ml) butter
6 tbsp (90 ml) maple syrup
3 cups (750 ml) sifted icing sugar
1/3 cup (75 ml) chopped walnuts
whole walnuts for garnish

Cream the butter mixing in maple syrup; add sugar gradually and beat to an even consistency. Spread a portion of icing on bottom cake, sprinkle with chopped nuts. Place second cake on the first. Frost the complete cake and garnish with a whole walnuts.

MAPLE CUPCAKES

An English pastry originally, cupcakes are back in fashion and the happy craze would not be complete without a touch of maple. These tasty cupcakes can be iced and decorated in any number of ways–let your imagination go wild!

1/4 cup (60 ml) butter, softened
1/4 cup (60 ml) sugar
1/2 cup (125 ml) maple syrup
2 eggs
1/4 cup (60 ml) yogurt with maple
1+1/3 cups (330 ml) flour
2 tsp baking powder
pinch of salt
1/4 cup (60 ml) maple flakes (or chopped walnuts)

FROSTING
1/2 cup (125 ml) cream cheese or ricotta
3 tbsp (45 ml) maple syrup

Preheat oven to 375°F (190°C).

Cream together butter and sugar. Gradually add the maple syrup, eggs and yogurt. In a bowl, mix flour, baking powder and salt. Stir the liquid ingredients into dry ingredients and add maple flakes (or walnuts). Drop paper cupcake cups in a muffin tin and fill cups with batter. Bake 20 minutes. In a bowl, combine frosting ingredients. Let the cupcakes cool before frosting.

DECORATION: You can sprinkle cupcakes with maple flakes, coloured sugar bits, or mini chocolate chips. Just make sure they are as pretty as they are delicious!

APPLE MAPLE SYRUP MUFFINS

Juicy and sweet, McIntosh apples have long held the lion's share of the market in Québec. Today, Macs share the shelves with other tasty varieties. For this recipe, we chose Cortland apples with their fragrant white flesh that retains its shape when cooked.

2 cups (500 ml) flour
1 tbsp baking powder
1/2 tsp cinnamon
pinch of salt
3/4 cup (180 ml) maple syrup
1 tbsp sunflower oil
2 eggs
1 1/4 cups (310 ml) unsweetened applesauce
1/2 cup (125 ml) dried apples, diced
1/2 cup (125 ml) walnuts

Preheat oven to 375°F (190°C).

In a bowl, combine flour, baking powder, cinnamon and salt. Set aside. In another bowl, whisk together maple syrup and oil. Add eggs and applesauce. Stir in dry ingredients and dried apples; stir until the dough is moist. Add nuts. Do not over mix. Spoon batter into oiled muffin tins. Bake about 20 minutes.

Makes 12-15 muffins.

TOFU MAPLE MUFFINS WITH OAT BRAN

These not-too-sweet muffins are perfect for breakfast. If you want them sweeter, slightly increase the amount of maple syrup in the recipe.

1 1/2 cups (375 ml) whole wheat pastry flour
1 cup (250 ml) oat bran
1 tbsp baking powder
3/4 cup (180 ml) golden raisins
1/2 cup (125 ml) silken tofu
1 egg
1/3 cup (80 ml) sunflower oil
1/2 cup (125 ml) maple syrup
1/2 cup (125 ml) milk

Preheat oven to 375°F (190°C).

In a bowl, mix flour, oat bran, baking powder and raisins. In a blender process tofu, egg, oil, maple syrup and milk. Incorporate liquid mixture into dry ingredients. Spoon into oiled muffin tins. Bake 20 minutes.

Makes 12 medium size muffins.

DID YOU KNOW... ?

MAPLE SYRUP IN TIN CANS DOES NOT HAVE AN EXPIRATION DATE. AS LONG AS THE SYRUP MAKES NO CONTACT WITH AIR, IT WON'T SPOIL AND THE SYRUP CAN BE KEPT AT ROOM TEMPERATURE FOR A FEW YEARS. ONCE THE CAN IS OPENED, IT MUST BE REFRIGERATED AND WILL KEEP FOR SEVERAL MONTHS IN AN AIRTIGHT CONTAINER. THE FREEZER, HOWEVER, IS THE BEST PLACE TO STORE AN OPENED CONTAINER FOR LONGER PERIODS.

SOURCE: FEDERATION OF QUÉBEC MAPLE SYRUP PRODUCERS.

540 ml
Sirop d'érable

MAPLE SUGAR BRETON SHORTBREAD COOKIES

Anyone who loves unique and exquisite desserts must get to know **Patrice Demers**, pastry chef at **Newtown** restaurant in Montréal. His creativity has managed to make the fine art of *pâtisserie* accessible to both beginners and the experienced gourmet. This recipe is from his cookbook *La carte des desserts* (Éditions de l'Homme).

4 egg yolks
1 1/2 cups (160 g) maple sugar
1 1/2 cups (225 g) flour
1 tbsp baking powder
2/3 cup + 2 tbsp (160 g) salted butter, softened

With an electric mixer, beat the egg yolks and sugar until the mixture is frothy. Sift together dry ingredients; add to egg mixture along with butter. Mix just enough to obtain a consistent mixture. Place dough on a sheet of parchment paper, cover with a second sheet then, using a rolling pin, roll out dough to a thickness of 1/2 inch (1 1/2 cm). Allow to set in refrigerator. Cut the cold shortbreads with stainless steel cutters and place cutters with dough on a baking sheet covered with parchment paper or on an oven-safe silicon mat. Bake the shortbreads in the steel cutters at 325°F (160°C) for about 12 minutes. Turn out the shortbreads while still warm by gently lifting off cutters.

For beautifully textured shortbreads, it's important to refrigerate the dough. You can even freeze the dough and bake straight from the freezer.

MAPLE SCONES

Well what do you know! You can enjoy scones with maple syrup at a chic little English café called Rose Bakery, rue des Martyrs-in Paris! Inspired by the recipe found in the wonderful book *Breakfast, Lunch & Tea*, these scones by **Julie** of the **Librairie Gourmande** bookstore in Montréal will be a hit at your Sunday brunch.

1/2 cup (125 ml) maple syrup
1/3 cup (80 ml) milk
2 1/2 cups (625 ml) all-purpose flour
1 tbsp baking powder
pinch of salt
3/4 cup + 1 tbsp (190 ml) cold butter, diced
1 egg, beaten

Preheat oven to 350°F (180°C).

In a bowl, combine maple syrup and milk. In another bowl, combine flour, baking powder and salt. Add butter and work until mixture turns to coarse crumbs. Make a well in centre, add liquid and combine using a fork. Finish by kneading by hand. Flour a work surface and roll out dough to 1 inch (2 1/2 cm) thick. Cut into triangles or use a cookie cutter. Place the scones on a baking sheet lined with parchment paper. Beat egg and brush over scones. Bake about 25 minutes.

Makes about a dozen scones.

CRISPY MAPLE MACAROONS

Jérôme Ferrer, chef-owner of the restaurant **Europea** in downtown Montréal, cooks with maple syrup–as much for glazing a duck or fillet of fish as for making his heavenly desserts. These maple macaroons, which are found on the restaurant's menu, are one of his best-loved creations according to dessert aficionados.

MERINGUE
1 1/4 cups (300 g) sugar
5 tsp water
4 egg whites

SHELL
2 1/3 cups (300 g) ground almonds
2 cups (300 g) icing sugar
4 egg whites

MAPLE CREAM
1 tbsp or 1 packet unflavoured gelatin
3 tbsp cold water
3/4 cup (180 ml) maple syrup
3 egg yolks
1 tbsp sugar
2 cups (500 ml) cream (35%)

MERINGUE: Combine sugar and water, then cook in a saucepan until candy thermometer shows 250°F (120°C). In a bowl, beat until stiff the 4 egg whites and cooked sugar. Let cool.

SHELL: In a bowl, mix the ground almonds and icing sugar. Stir this mixture into the other 4 egg whites and beat for 3 minutes. Gently fold in the meringue. On a baking sheet lined with parchment paper, form macaroons using a pastry bag or a small spoon. Allow to sit about 30 minutes at room temperature so a crust forms, then bake in oven preheated to 350°F (180°C) for 6-7 minutes. Cool, then place in a slightly humid cloth and refrigerate.

MAPLE CREAM: Soak gelatin in the cold water. Heat the maple syrup over low heat and stir in gelatin. Remove from heat. In a bowl, whisk egg yolks with sugar until frothy. Stir egg yolk mixture into maple syrup mixture. Whip the cream, add to the mix and let stand for one to two hours in the refrigerator. Spread cream on the bottom of a macaroon and cover with another macaroon. Refrigerate 5 to 6 hours before serving.

CRÈME BRÛLÉE WITH LAVENDER *À LA MOUTON NOIR*

Le Mouton Noir is a legendary restaurant in Baie Saint-Paul, in the gorgeous Charlevoix region of Québec. The hotel-restaurant was a Mecca for Québécois pop stars and hippies in the seventies, but more recently it has become a major centre of *haute cuisine*, under the direction of chef **Thierry Ferré**. "This crème brûlée, which we serve at the restaurant, contains maple syrup and to accentuate the flavour, I add a few drops more after the sugar has caramelized."

1 cup (250 ml) cream (35%)
1/2 cup (125 ml) milk
4 egg yolks
2 tbsp maple syrup
3 tbsp sugar
12 lavender flowers
1/4 cup (60 ml) maple sugar

In a saucepan over low heat, heat milk and cream. In a bowl, combine the yolks, sugar and maple syrup. Gently whisk in the warm cream and milk. Divide evenly pouring into *crème brûlée* ramekins and sprinkle with lavender flowers. Place ramekins in a double boiler with 2 inches of lukewarm water. Carefully cook in preheated oven at 300°F (150°C) for 20-30 minutes. Remove from oven and take *crème brûlées* out of double boiler. Cool. Sprinkle with maple sugar and burn with a blowtorch until caramelized.

MAPLE ICE CREAM

Specially created for the annual culinary contest **Les Créatifs de l'érable** (Québec's gourmet multi-regional gastronomic 'maple road'), this ice cream with its subtle taste of burnt caramel won a top prize in 2009. Throughout the year you can taste this rich, sweet treat at the boutique **Havre-aux-Glaces**–the 'ice-cream haven'–run by **Robert** and **Richard Lachapelle** at the Jean-Talon Market in Montréal.

3/4 cup (180 ml) cream (35%)
1 cup (200 g) maple sugar
6-7 egg yolks
1 1/3 cup (330 ml) milk

Heat cream and set aside. In a saucepan, cook dry maple sugar, stirring constantly, until a candy thermometer registers 310°F (153°C). Remove from heat and slowly pour hot cream over the caramel sugar, stirring constantly; this is to *décuire*, or correct the temperature. Refrigerate overnight.

The next day, mix the egg yolks and milk. In a saucepan, heat the caramel and add the egg mixture. Heat, stirring constantly, and cook until a candy thermometer shows 170°F (85°C). Cool by placing pan in bath of ice water. Churn in an ice-cream maker.

MAPLE SORBET

2 1/4 cups + 3 tbsp (600 ml) maple syrup
1 1/2 cups + 2 tbsp (400 ml) water

Mix well. Allow to 'sleep' overnight in refrigerator. Churn the next day in an ice-cream maker. An astonishing flavour of maple on snow.

MAPLE-CARAMEL PECANS

1/2 cup (125 ml) maple syrup
1/4 cup (60 ml) sugar
1/4 cup (60 ml) water
1 1/2 cups (375 ml) pecans
pinch of sea salt

In a saucepan, bring to boil maple syrup, sugar and water. Add pecans and stir until mixture crystallizes. As a final touch, add sea salt. Allow to cool on a baking sheet lined with parchment paper.

GRANOLA WITH MAPLE AND APPLE

A veritable smorgasbord of energy to start the day. Make sure to only add the dried fruits after cooking the granola, otherwise they will burn.

2 cups (500 ml) rolled oats
1/2 cup (125 ml) wheat germ
1/2 cup (125 ml) unsweetened shredded coconut
1/2 cup (125 ml) unsalted sunflower seeds
1 tbsp powdered milk
pinch of salt
3/4 cup (180 ml) maple syrup
2 tbsp sunflower oil
1/2 cup (125 ml) dried apples, diced
1/2 cup (125 ml) dried cranberries
mixed spices: 1/2 tsp nutmeg + 1 tsp ginger

Preheat oven to 300°F (160°C).

Mix spices and set aside. In a large bowl, combine rolled oats, wheat germ, coconut, sunflower seeds, milk powder and salt. In a saucepan, heat without boiling maple syrup and oil. Remove from heat and add spices. Pour syrup mixture over cereal and mix well. Spread mixture on a baking sheet lined with parchment paper. Bake 30-40 minutes, stirring every 10 minutes. Remove from oven and transfer to a large bowl. Add dried fruits; mix well. Let cool completely. The granola will keep for several weeks in an airtight container.

MAPLE CARAMEL CHOCOLATES

The recipe for these mouth-watering chocolates is one of many delicious secrets from the boutique **Chocolats Privilège** in Montréal's Jean-Talon Market.

5/8 cup (140 ml) maple syrup
1/2 cup (125 ml) cream (35%)
8 tsp corn syrup
1 3/4 oz (50 g) milk chocolate

Cook the maple syrup, cream and corn syrup until candy thermometer shows 220°F (105°C). Cool to 158°F (70°C), then add the milk chocolate. If desired: pour into maple-leaf shaped chocolate molds. Allow to stand for 12 hours.

Pour over with melted chocolate; allow to set and then carefully remove from molds. Makes 24 beautiful chocolate maple leaves.

MAPLE CARAMEL

We asked **Michelle Marek**, head pastry chef at both **Laloux** restaurant and **POP! bar à vin** to prepare for us something sinfully sweet with maple syrup, cream and a touch of butter...*et voilà!* You'll eat this treat straight out of the jar or spread thick on toast.

1/2 cup + 2 tbsp (150 ml) maple sugar
1/4 cup (60 ml) salted butter
3/4 cup + 2 tbsp (210 ml) cream (35%)
1/4 cup (60 ml) maple syrup
1/2 cup + 2 tbsp (150 ml) granulated sugar

Combine all ingredients except for white sugar; set aside. In a deep skillet, melt the white sugar and allow to cook to a dark caramel color. *Décuire*, or correct the temperature by carefully pouring in the maple-cream mixture. Be careful, since the caramel sugar is at a much higher temperature and may cause sudden bubbling. Stir vigorously.

When the bubbles have subsided, cook, stirring gently until candy thermometer shows 225°F (110°C). Pour the maple spread into a jam jar and allow to cool.

DID YOU KNOW... ?

YOU CAN USE MAPLE PRODUCTS TO REPLACE SUGAR IN ANY RECIPE. MAPLE SUGAR CAN BE SUBSTITUTED FOR AN EQUAL AMOUNT OF WHITE SUGAR, WHILE FOR EACH CUP (250 ML) OF SYRUP USED, SIMPLY CUT BACK ABOUT 1/4 CUP (60 ML) OF THE LIQUID (WATER, MILK OR JUICE) REQUIRED IN THE RECIPE.

SOURCE: FEDERATION OF QUÉBEC MAPLE SYRUP PRODUCERS.

MAPLE FUDGE

The Québécois definitely have a sweet tooth and this fudge is a kind of soul food. There are as many maple fudge recipes as there are *grand-mères* in the province! Here is a simple one. To ensure that it melts in the mouth, don't overcook it, since this will make the fudge harden too quickly and become brittle.

2 cups (500 ml) maple sugar
1 cup (250 ml) cream (35%)
1/2 cup (125 ml) chopped Québec butternuts
(or regular walnuts)

Mix maple sugar and cream in a saucepan large enough to allow a vigorous boil without overflowing. On low heat, melt sugar, stirring gently. When sugar is completely melted, cook over fairly high heat without stirring until candy thermometer shows 238°F (115°C), or until a small amount of mixture thrown into ice water makes a soft ball. Remove from heat and let cool. Add nuts and stir with a wooden spoon until the sugar begins to lose luster. Pour onto a baking sheet lined with parchment paper. Cut into squares before the fudge is completely cool.

ZABAGLIONE WITH BERRIES AND MAPLE

2 cups (500 ml) fresh berries
(e.g. strawberries, raspberries, blueberries or blackberries)
2 tbsp maple sugar or maple flakes
3 egg yolks
1/3 cup (80 ml) maple syrup
3 tbsp white port

In a bowl, combine berries and maple sugar and let stand ten minutes. Divide among the ramekins or glasses. Set aside. In the top of a double boiler, combine remaining ingredients in a stainless steel mixing bowl. Place over a pan of simmering water and whisk constantly for 5 minutes, until the mixture swells and becomes creamy. Pour over berries and place under the broiler until barely browned.

VERRINE OF MAPLE, CURRY AND COCONUT

Within the new discipline of molecular gastronomy, based on the scientific harmonizing of flavours, internationally award-winning Québec sommelier and author **François Chartier** has devoted considerable research into "the aromatic sap of Québec identity." Chartier informs us that the signature aroma of maple syrup is the molecule sotolon. Interestingly, this potent compound is also key to the aroma of curry. Sotolon combines with and complements foods containing lactones, one of which is coconut.

This artfully arranged fruit cup, or *verrine*, brings together all three ingredients as per the information found in Chartier's bestseller *Papilles et Molécules*–winner of the prestigious "Best Cookbook in the World" award, innovation category, at the *World Cookbook Awards 2010* in Paris.

MAPLE GELATIN
2 wafers of gelatin (or 2 tsp powdered gelatin)*
1/2 cup (125 ml) amber maple syrup
3/4 cup (180 ml) water

APPLE-CURRY MIXTURE
1 Granny Smith apple, finely diced
2 tbsp amber maple syrup
1/4 tsp curry powder

COCONUT MILK MOUSSE
1/2 cup (125 ml) coconut milk
1/2 cup (125 ml) cream (35%)
2 tbsp maple syrup

For gelatin in wafers or sheets, soak wafers in enough water to cover. In a small saucepan, boil the maple syrup and water. Drain the gelatin; add to the hot maple liquid and dissolve. Cool 10 minutes then pour into 4 glasses. Refrigerate at least 6 hours. *If using powdered gelatin, soak in 3 tbsp cold water until it swells up, then dissolve in the pan with hot maple syrup and water.

Combine apples, maple syrup and curry powder. Set aside in refrigerator.

For the coconut mousse, mix the coconut milk, cream, and maple syrup. Filter through a sieve and pour into pressurized Chantilly cream canister. Refrigerate until ready to serve.

When serving, divide the diced apples into the 4 glasses of maple jelly and top with coconut-maple mousse from the canister.

MARBLED MAPLE RICE PUDDING

This elegant take on traditional rice pudding incorporates flavours of early summer in the form of strawberry and rhubarb.

RICE PUDDING
1/3 cup (80 ml) arborio rice, rinsed and drained
2 2/3 cups (660 ml) milk
1/2 vanilla bean, split and scraped
1/3 cup (80 ml) maple syrup
1 egg, separated

STRAWBERRY RHUBARB COMPOTE (see page 37)

In a saucepan, add the rice, milk, vanilla and maple syrup. Bring to just boiling and simmer 20-30 minutes, stirring frequently. When the rice is cooked, add the egg yolk and mix. Continue cooking 2 minutes, remove from heat and let cool. Whisk egg white and stir into rice. Refrigerate.

To serve, divide the rice pudding and strawberry-rhubarb compote (see recipe page 37) into serving glasses in alternating layers. Finish with a layer of rice pudding.

DRINKS

A LEXICON OF LIQUIDS

The Amerindians have always known about the secret of maple 'water.' Over time, a whole lexicon of words has evolved to describe different liquids derived from the sugar maple.

Bagosse des sucres: An alcoholic drink made by fermenting a blend of wheat and grapes that is distilled in the sugar shack.

Caribou de cabane: An alcoholic drink made from a pint of red wine to ten ounces of whisky that is cut with concentrated sap taken from the *bouilleuse*, or primary kettle.

Eau d'érable: The term used for the clear, delicately flavoured sap of the earlier half of the sap run. When the sugar-maker uses the word sève, it refers to the more bitter sap running near the end of sugar season that does make as good a product.

Sève: Sugar maple sap that runs at the end of the season. It gives a dark-coloured syrup that is not of as high a quality.

Sirop de bourgeon: A syrup with a 'greenish flavour of the buds' or bark. This does not last more than a day or two and the cause of it is related to weather. It can happen at any time during the sugar-making season, especially at the start if the run comes on too suddenly or after two consecutive days of very warm weather.

Sirop de sève: Syrup from the end of the season having a more bitter taste. Only with difficulty can it be made into a hard sugar, but it is excellent for making a delicious soft sugar that is called *sucre à la crème*, on account of its texture.

Thé de sève: Tea that is made using maple sap instead of water.

Terminology from the book *Le temps des sucres* by ethnologist Jean-Claude Dupont (Éditions GID, 2004), by permission of the author.

MANGO-MAPLE TOFU SMOOTHIE

Chef **Marie-Sophie Picard** of the **Auberge du Mange-Grenouille** in Bic, Québec, is always first in line each spring to enjoy maple taffy on snow, that most joyful of spring pleasures. She has a lot of fun cooking with maple products that she describes as 'the flagship ingredient' of Québec cuisine.

3/4 cup (180 ml) fresh or frozen mango, cubed
3/4 cup (180 ml) soft tofu
3/4 cup (180 ml) plain yogurt
1/2 cup (125ml) soy milk
2 tbsp maple syrup
pinch of ground cardamom or cinnamon, to taste (optional)

In a blender, add cubes of mango, tofu, yogurt. Process until smooth. Add remaining ingredients and process for a minute or two. Pour into refrigerated glasses. Garnish with fresh fruit.

DID YOU KNOW... ?

IN QUÉBEC, ACCORDING THE GOVERNMENT'S COMMISSION OF TOPONYMY (PLACE NAMES), YOU'LL FIND MORE THAN 350 STREETS NAMED EITHER *RUE DES ÉRABLES*, *CHEMIN DES ÉRABLES*, *AVENUE DES ÉRABLES* OR *ROUTE DES ÉRABLES*.

(SOURCE: GOVERNMENT OF QUÉBEC TOPONYMY COMMISSION - WWW.TOPONYMIE.GOUV.QC.CA)

BLUEBERRY SMOOTHIE À *L'ÉRABLE*

1 1/2 cups (375 ml) fresh or frozen blueberries
1 cup (250 ml) plain yogurt
1 cup (250 ml) milk
1/4 cup (60 ml) maple syrup

In a blender, add all ingredients and process at high speed. Add some ice if you're using fresh blueberries. Pour into refrigerated glasses.

CAFFÈ LATTE À *L'ÉRABLE*

According to sommelier **François Chartier** (see page 121), author of *Papilles et Molécules*, "if you harmonize maple syrup, which is rich in cyclotene, with coffee, which also contains an ethyl-cyclotene, the coffee effectively amplifies the flavours of the maple syrup." How irresistible!

1 cup (250 ml) evaporated milk (2%)
1/4 cup (60 ml) maple syrup
2 cups (500 ml) hot coffee

In a saucepan, heat milk and maple syrup over medium heat, stirring constantly. Froth the milk (using steam attachment on cappuccino machine). Pour into hot coffee.

MAPLE TODDY

Ethné, the lovely Trinidadian co-owner of the boutique **La Dépense** in the Jean-Talon Market, Montréal, offers up this heartwarming toddy recipe. It's full of Caribbean warmth and flavours, to be enjoyed in winter by the fireside.

1 1/2 oz (45 ml) dark rum
1 1/2 oz (45 ml) dark maple syrup
1 tbsp butter (salted)
a few drops of lime juice
3 drops Angostura bitters (optional)
pinch of grated nutmeg or tonka bean
1/2 cup (125 ml) boiling water

Pour all ingredients into a cup. Stir well until butter is melted. Cheers!

SPRINGTIME GIN & TONIC

Long ago maple sap used to be consumed as a cleansing spring tonic by the Amerindians. Since sap is not available in stores, maple syrup and club soda work nicely, too. The name is a play on gin and tonic, here literally a gin tonic. The lemon and chili are very cleansing, and they brighten up the flavours while tempering the sweetness of the maple. Light, tart and refreshing, it's a perfect pick-me-up at any time of the year, especially so in springtime.

In a gin and tonic glass, pour
1 1/2 oz (45 ml) gin
1 oz (30 ml) lemon juice
3/4 oz (25 ml) maple syrup
2 pinches Espelette chili peppers

Dilute with club soda or sparkling water. Add ice cubes and garnish the glass with a slice of lemon.

ONE HUNDRED *CRÉATIFS DE L'ÉRABLE* FOUR SEASONS ONE GOURMET ROAD

JOIN THE MAPLE GOURMET ROAD!

From Abitibi-Témiscamingue to the Eastern Townships, from the Charlevoix region to the Magdalen Islands, from the Lower St. Lawrence down to the greater Montréal region, the Maple Gourmet Road (*La Route de l'érable*) showcases all of the magic of maple cuisine from the four corners of Québec. Taste a sparkling wine perfumed with maple or a daring chef's *foie gras* with maple jelly. You will be enchanted while exploring the Maple Gourmet Road.

DISCOVER THE WORK OF 100 TALENTED ARTISANS

Carefully selected by the Federation of Québec Maple Syrup Producers, the 100 *Créatifs de l'érable* include Québec's top chefs and artisans. Overflowing with imagination, these innovators have taken maple syrup cuisine to a whole new level for their clientele, in surprisingly flavourful new ways. Explore and indulge at any time of the year!

MAPLE AMBASSADORS ABROAD

In Québec, you will find Créatifs all along the Maple Gourmet Road, in every corner of the province. But if you look further, you'll find Créatifs in France and Japan as well, putting their boundless creativity to work to create new taste experiences.

To arrange your own adventure on the Maple Gourmet Road, and to discover a whole new perspective on Québec's rich and delicious culinary heritage, visit the website of *La Route de l'érable* at www.laroutedelerable.ca.

OUR GENEROUS PARTNERS WHO HELPED THIS BOOK INTO BEING

CUIZIN
7070 Henri-Julien, Marché Jean-Talon, Montréal (Québec) • Tel. 514-273-9339 • www.cuizin.ca

LA DÉPENSE
7070 Henri-Julien, Marché Jean-Talon, Montréal (Québec) • Tel. 514-273-1118 • www.epicesdecru.com

LALOUX
250 ave. des Pins Est, Montréal (Québec) • Tel. 514-287-9127 • www.laloux.com

PRINCE NOIR
7070 Henri-Julien, Marché Jean-Talon, Montréal (Québec) • Tel. 514-906-1110

CRÉATIFS DE L'ÉRABLE

AUBERGE DES GLACIS
46 Route de la Tortue, Saint-Eugène-de-l'Islet (Québec) • Tel. 418-247-7486 • www.aubergedesglacis.com

AUBERGE DU MANGE-GRENOUILLE
148 Sainte-Cécile, Le Bic (Québec) • Tel. 418-736-5656 • www.aubergedumangegrenouille.qc.ca

CHOCOLATS PRIVILÈGE INC.
7070 Henri-Julien, Marché Jean-Talon, Montréal (Québec) • Tel. 514-276-7070 • www.chocolatsprivilege.com

CORNELLIER TRAITEUR
5354 St. Lawrence Blvd., Montréal (Québec) • Tel. 514-272-8428 • www.cornelliertraiteur.com

ÉRABLIÈRE CHARBONNEAU
45 Chemin du Sous-Bois, Mont-Saint-Grégoire (Québec) • Tel. 450-347-9090 • www.erablierecharbonneau.qc.ca

EUROPEA
1227 de la Montagne, Montréal (Québec) • Tel. 514-398-9229 • www.europea.ca

HAVRE-AUX-GLACES
7070 Henri-Julien, Marché Jean-Talon, Montréal (Québec) • Tel. 514-278-8696

MOUTON NOIR
43 rue Sainte-Anne, Baie Saint-Paul, (Québec) • Tel. 418-240-3030 • www.laloux.com

BIBLIOGRAPHY

BENOIT, Jehane, *Encyclopédie de la cuisine de Jehane Benoit*, Éditions Mirabel, 1991

BOISVENUE, Lorraine, *Le guide de la cuisine traditionnelle québécoise*, Éditions Stanké, 1979

CARRARINI, Rose, *Breakfast, Lunch & Tea*, Éditions Phaidon, 2007

CHARTIER, François, *Papilles et Molécules, La science aromatique des aliments et des vins*, Éditions La Presse, 2009

DEMERS, Patrice, *La carte des desserts*, Éditions de l'Homme, 2009

DE VIENNE, Ethné et Philippe, *La cuisine et le goût des épices*, Éditions Trécarré, 2007

DUPONT, Jean-Claude, *Le temps des sucres*, Éditions GID, 2004

FERRER, Jérôme, *Le secret des sauces*, Éditions La Presse, 2008

GLOUTNEZ, Germaine, *La cuisine québécoise*, Éditions Bert-Hold, 1979,

HUOT, Juliette, *Mes meilleures recettes aux pommes*, Éditions La Presse, 1972

LAMBERT, Michel, *Histoire de la cuisine familiale du Québec, Volume 1, Ses origines autochtones et européennes*, Éditions GID, 2006

Magazine *Châtelaine / Chatelaine* Magazine, www.chatelaine.com.

Note: Every recipe this cookbook was formulated for four servings except where indicated.

With the exception of a few recipes, notably the pastries, metric measures have been included as volumetric instead of weight measures.

The photos of the *cabane à sucre* in this book were taken at the Érablière Charbonneau in Mont Saint-Grégoire where we greatly enjoyed all the warm hospitality.

INDEX

HEARTFELT THANKS...

To Antoine Ross Trempe, editor-in-chief at Cardinal, for his valuable input at every step of the way in this project, and especially for having believed in this amazing collaboration.

To Céline Comeau, our food stylist, an extra-special thank you for tirelessly testing dozens of recipes to ensure that we picked the very best.

To the careful eye of Dominique Lafond who knew so well how to position her camera in just the right places as each dish came out of the oven.

To my dear friends at the Jean-Talon Market who so generously supplied so many maple-sweet recipes: Philippe and Ethné de Vienne from *La Dépense*, Michel Boulais of *Prince Noir*, Ludovic Fresse from *Chocolats Privilège*, and Robert and Richard Lachapelle from *Havre-aux-Glaces*.

To my friend Donald from *CuiZin* who furnished the accessories to make each dish look so marvellous.

To Julie and Marie-Neige, an extra-special thank you to you both for having been so dependable and supportive at *Librairie Gourmande* during this demanding period during which the book took shape.

To my sister Suzanne, the designer, who is always there to create beautiful images for my projects, in particular this book.

To Gab at Groupe Oracio Design for her exemplary patience.

To my children, Jeanne and Pierre-Louis, who were the first-round tasters and who make me so proud with their discerning palates.

To Dad and Mum, I know you're keeping your eye on me!

SWEET NOTES